WATER
SAVING
TIPS

HB
HINKLER
BOOKS

Writer and editor: Louise Coulthard
Designer: Katy Wall
Prepress: Graphic Print Group
Typesetter: Midland Typesetters
Image credits: iStockphoto.com: © Steve Dibblee, Sviatlana Dziamidava,
Brandon Seidel, Ufuk Zivana, Jolande Gerritsen
Dreamstime.com: © Uschi Hering, Joachim Angeltun
Cover image: Inmagine.com

365 Water Saving Tips
Published in 2006 by Hinkler Books Pty Ltd
45–55 Fairchild Street
Heatherton VIC 3202 Australia
www.hinklerbooks.com

© Hinkler Books Pty Ltd 2006

10 9 8 7 6 5 4 3 2 1
11 10 09 08 07

ISBN: 978 1 7418 1334 0

Printed and bound in Australia

CONTENTS

INTRODUCTION ℹ

Water is a precious resource

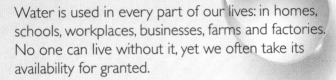

Water is used in every part of our lives: in homes, schools, workplaces, businesses, farms and factories. No one can live without it, yet we often take its availability for granted.

Living in the driest populated continent on Earth, Australians need to be especially aware of how we use water. Our country is regularly affected by drought and water shortages, meaning we need to rethink our water consumption and usage. With water resources decreasing all the time, it is vital that people realise how scarce water is and how their actions can affect water storage levels.

Everyone can play an important part in reducing water consumption. The good news is that even small changes to your everyday life can have a major effect on reducing water wastage. It's really easy to save water, and everyone can do it! Best of all, you'll be saving one of the world's most precious natural resources and ensuring that it will be available for future generations.

> **DID YOU KNOW?**
>
> 97.5% of the water on Earth is salt water and 2.5% is fresh water.
> Only 0.3% of that fresh water is available from reservoirs, rivers and lakes.
> 30% of fresh water comes from groundwater.
> The rest of the world's fresh water is inaccessible, stored in glaciers, ice sheets, the Arctic and Antarctic and as snow on mountains.

Set your goal!

The challenge is to reduce your water usage by at least ten per cent every water billing cycle. Find your most recent water bill and look at the total of litres you've used. Work out ten per cent (or more!) of that figure and make it your goal to reduce the amount of water used by your household in the next billing cycle by that figure.

Of course, you might find that your water usage varies depending on the season, so you may want to use the total from a corresponding period of the previous year. If you don't have your old bills, your water provider should be able to provide you with the correct figure.

If you are renting, check with your landlord or real estate agent to see if they can provide you with the correct details of your water usage.

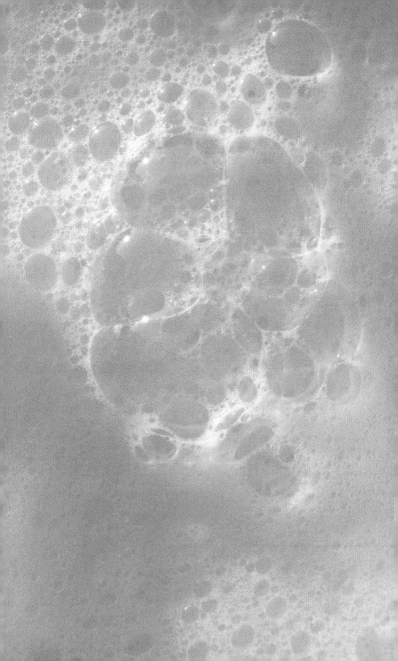

BATHROOM

General

1 Install AAA-rated or the new WELS (Water Efficiency Labelling and Standards) three-star flow control valves and aerators in your taps. A flow control valve regulates and reduces the amount of water that comes through the tap or shower. An aerator fits in the end of a tap and aerates the water, giving the sensation of a higher flow rate while reducing the amount of water that flows through.

2 Ensure the plugs in your bath and basin don't leak. Buy new plugs if the existing ones don't completely seal the drain.

3 An instantaneous water heater will ensure water stays hot from the hot water system to the bathroom, reducing the need to waste water as you wait for it to heat up.

4 Using single lever taps means that you can find your preferred temperature faster, reducing the amount of water wasted.

> **DID YOU KNOW?**
> Approximately 14–25% of a household's water usage occurs in the bathroom.

> **DID YOU KNOW?**
> Flow control valves and aerator taps can reduce water flow by up to 50%.

Basin

5 Don't leave the basin tap running while you brush your teeth. Instead, fill a glass for rinsing your mouth and the basin.

6 When soaping your hands, turn off the water while you lather.

7 Don't leave the tap running while having a shave. Half-fill the basin with water for rinsing your face and the razor.

> **DID YOU KNOW?**
>
> The basin tap can use up to 15 litres of water a minute.

8 Reuse tap water by keeping a container in your basin. This can later be used on garden beds and pot plants.

9 Look into purchasing taps fitted with infra-red sensors that only run the water while your hands are in front of the sensor.

> **DID YOU KNOW?**
>
> Washing your hands can use up to 5 litres of water.

Shower

10 Take shorter showers. Having a shower in four minutes instead of ten can save tens of thousands of litres of water a year.

11 One of the best ways to save water in the bathroom is to install low-flow water efficient shower heads. Look for at least WELS three-star or AAA-rated shower heads, but check that they'll work with your plumbing.

12 Before you shower, set an alarm on a clock or kitchen timer to sound after three or four minutes to alert you to finish up.

13 Have a navy shower! Used by sailors to conserve water on sea voyages, this is a great water saver. Simply turn on the shower, wet your body, turn off the water, then soap, shampoo and lather, and turn on the shower long enough to rinse off.

14 Don't use power showers. These use more water than conventional showers and can use more water than it takes to fill a deep bath.

15 Instead of shaving your legs in the shower, fill a container of water and use it to lather up and shave before you get in. Rinse off as part of your regular shower.

16 Don't run the shower at full pressure while you wait for the water to warm up. Keep it at a trickle and you'll use less water.

17 Catch water that's wasted while the shower warms up in a bucket or container. Use the surplus water to water plants, for cleaning or to wash the car. You can even keep the bucket there to catch water as you shower. Just remember to check your soap is safe to use on plants.

18 When adjusting shower temperature, only turn the water down instead of up. Turning down the cold tap will just as effectively warm up the shower as turning up the hot tap.

DID YOU KNOW?

A low-flow shower uses 9 litres of water a minute.

Bath

19 If possible, take showers instead of baths. An average bath uses a lot more water than a short shower.

DID YOU KNOW?

A four minute shower with a low-flow shower head uses around 36 litres of water while a full bath uses about 150 litres.

20 If you have some family members who like baths and others who prefer to shower, let the showerers go first. While they shower, plug the bath so that it fills using the shower water instead of running bath water from the tap.

21 If you're renovating or building a new property, choose a smaller bathtub that uses less water.

22 Put the plug in the bath tub before you start to fill it, and then adjust the temperature as it fills. This prevents wasting water down the drain while you wait for it to heat up.

23 Check the bath as it fills so it doesn't overflow. Don't let water end up going down the drain or on the bathroom floor!

24 Only fill the bath to a level that's appropriate for your needs. If you're bathing children or even pets, you won't need a full bath.

25 Use a baby bath to wash babies and toddlers instead of filling the bath tub.

26 If you have young children, bathe them together to avoid running the bath several times.

27 Used bathwater needn't go down the drain. If your soaps and shampoos are suitable, reuse bathwater on the garden or to wash the car. If necessary, check with your local nursery to see if bathwater can be used safely your plants.

28 Replace a single-flush toilet with a dual-flush toilet and use the half-flush option whenever you can.

29 An old toilet's cistern holds up to twelve litres, several litres more than a newer toilet. If you don't wish to replace the whole toilet, install a new dual-flush cistern.

30 Flow restrictors and cistern savers (or toilet dams) can be installed to reduce the amount of water used in a single-flush toilet. A cistern saver is usually a bag or balloon-like device that can be purchased at any hardware store. It is placed in the cistern and fills up, preventing the water it holds from being flushed away. Alternatively, some people find that placing a brick or a two-litre capped plastic bottle filled with water or gravel in the cistern also works well as a water-displacing device. If you need two flushes to clear the bowl, try a smaller bottle or brick.

31 Install a small device to your toilet to reduce the volume of water each flush uses. A button inhibitor will ensure the toilet only flushes while the flush button is held down. Pushing down for a shorter duration means less water will be used per flush.

32 Ensure that the flush button or handle doesn't get stuck down after flushing. A stuck flusher allows the water to run constantly, potentially wasting thousands of litres. Replace it if it consistently gets stuck down.

33 Take the drastic step of not flushing every time you use the toilet! A Californian water campaign from the 1970s read, 'If it's yellow, let it mellow. If it's brown, flush it down.'

34 Check the water level in the cistern. Most toilets have a line, mark or raised section showing the ideal level. If the level is too high, adjust the float valve or ballcock.

DID YOU KNOW?

A new dual-flush cistern uses 9 litres for a full flush but less than 4.5 litres for a half flush.

until they warm up. This water can then be used to flush the toilet instead

35 Chlorine or bleach cistern tablets may damage rubber and plastic parts in the toilet, leading to leaks and wearing. Use an in-bowl toilet cleaner to avoid damage.

36 Don't flush away tissues and other rubbish in your toilet. Use a rubbish bin instead.

37 Use a bucket to save the cold water that comes out of the shower or taps

of going down the drain, saving the water in your cistern.

38 Set up your plumbing system so that rainwater and greywater can be used to flush the toilet.

39 Check for leaks around the base of the toilet bowl and ensure any cracks are repaired quickly.

40 Composting toilets and waterless toilets are available. Check with your local authority to see if these are permitted in your area and if they're suitable for your household.

DID YOU KNOW?

The amount of water that's used in one flush of a normal Western toilet is the equivalent to the total amount a person in the developing world uses in a whole day.

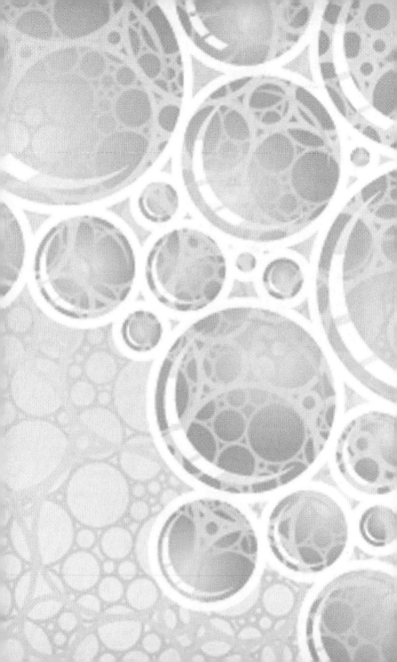

LAUNDRY

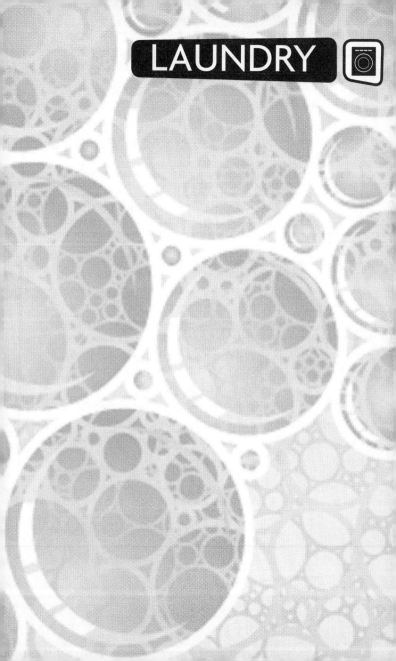

Washing machine

41 Ensure your washing machine is water efficient. Front-loading washing machines use less water than top loaders. Look for a model with an AAAAA or the new six-star rating, the highest water efficiency level.

42 Only use your washing machine when you have a full load, even if the machine has adjustable water levels.

43 If you must wash clothes with a less-than-full load, use a machine with a variable water volume setting and choose the minimum level of water needed per load. Some newer machines can select the appropriate water level automatically.

44 If your clothes aren't very dirty, use the shortest wash cycle available.

45 If your washing machine has one, use the suds-saver setting when you have more than one load to wash. This will not only save water, but also the amount of detergent you use.

46 Clothes washer hoses can become brittle and crack. Check them regularly to ensure they aren't leaking through any cracks or breaks.

DID YOU KNOW?

Older models of washing machines can use enough water each load to fill a bath.

47 Regularly check washing machine taps for drips and leaks.

48 Safety valves are available that shut off the water flow if the washing machine hose breaks or slips. While this reduces the amount of water wasted, it also stops flooding!

49 Pre-treating heavy stains before washing will reduce the chance that you'll need to re-wash clothes.

Hand washing

50 Install three-star or AAA-rated or higher flow control valves and aerators in your laundry trough taps.

51 If you are washing clothes by hand, use only as much water as you need in the laundry sink, bucket or tub.

52 When hand washing, rinse clothes in a separate tub, bucket or plugged sink instead of using a running tap.

53 Reuse the washing and rinsing water as much as possible if you have several rounds of hand washing to do.

54 Instead of using the woollens and delicates cycle on your washing machine, hand wash these items.

DID YOU KNOW?

Washing clothes in the laundry trough uses around 40 litres of water.

KITCHEN

General

55 Install three-star or AAA-rated or higher flow control valves and aerators in your kitchen taps.

56 It's easy to get distracted with other tasks in the kitchen and leave the water running. Make sure you turn off kitchen taps when they're not in use.

57 Instead of letting tap water run down the drain while you wait for it to cool, keep a bottle or jug of water in the fridge. You'll have cool water to drink and avoid wastage.

58 Compost your food scraps for your garden instead of running a garbage-disposal unit.

59 If you must use a garbage disposal unit, connect the outlet to a tank and use the water on your garden. The mulched vegetables and water are rich in nutrients.

60 Don't run your kitchen taps without plugging the sink or running it into a container. This water can then be used on pot plants or the garden.

61 While waiting for running water to cool down or warm up, catch it in a bottle or container and reuse it for kitchen tasks, on plants or as chilled drinking water.

62 Use just one glass each time you drink water over the course of the day. You'll reduce the amount of glasses you need to wash and the number of times you need to fill the sink or run the dishwasher.

63 Installing an instant water heater on your kitchen taps means you won't need to let the water run until it gets hot.

64 Place dropped ice blocks into a pot plant instead of the sink.

65 Don't use the ice-maker in your refrigerator. Use an ice block tray instead.

Dishwashers

66 Choose a water-efficient dishwasher with a high rating. Water-efficient dishwashers can use less than one litre of water for each place setting.

67 Only use your dishwasher when it is full of dishes. This uses less water than washing the same number of dishes in the sink.

68 Read your dishwasher manual and understand its settings. Many new dishwashers have half-load or economy settings and allow you to adjust the water level.

69 Use the rinse and hold setting on your dishwasher, if it has one. This reduces or removes the need to rinse your dishes in the kitchen sink before putting them in the dishwasher.

DID YOU KNOW?

A dishwasher uses around 20–50 litres per cycle.

70 Scrape plates clean instead of rinsing them. The food scraps can be scraped into a compost bin to be used on the garden.

71 Newer models of dishwashers are much better at cleaning than old ones. Most will effectively clean dishes without needing a pre-rinse.

72 Make sure your dishwasher has a safety valve installed to shut off the water if the dishwasher tap leaks or breaks. This stops flooding and saves water.

DID YOU KNOW?

A half-full sink holds around 12 litres.

Hand washing dishes

73 Try only half-filling the sink when washing dishes. Piling fewer dishes in the sink at a time means you'll need less water to cover them.

74 Start by washing the least dirty dishes first. This means the water won't get as dirty and will reduce the number of times you'll need to refill the sink, if at all.

75 Don't rinse dishes under a running tap. If you have a double sink, half-fill one side and use it to rinse the dishes. If you only have a single sink, fill a plastic tub or basin with rinsing water. This water can also be used on pot plants and the garden or for cleaning.

76 Another rinsing option is to wash all the dishes and stack them in a drying rack. Then use a container of water or, if your tap is equipped with one, a spray nozzle to rinse the dishes in the rack.

77 Instead of waiting for the hot water to warm up, boil a kettle of water to wash the dishes with. Add enough cold water until it reaches the desired temperature and don't add any more from the tap.

DID YOU KNOW?

Washing dishes by hand uses about 18 litres of water.

78 Save all your dishes until the evening and wash them in one go.

79 Only use as much detergent as you need. This will cut down the amount of foam, and therefore the amount of rinsing.

80 Don't rinse cooking pots and pans under a running tap while you scrape off cooked-on food. Instead, soak them in a small amount of water.

81 Use aluminium foil as a pan liner and reduce the amount of food build-up on cooking utensils, meaning you won't need to rinse them as much. Contact your local recycling service to see if the used foil can be recycled.

82 Soaking pots in a small amount of water as soon as you've finished cooking with them will prevent sauces and liquids drying on, thus making them harder to remove. Soaking will prevent you having to wash cookware multiple times to get it clean.

Cooking

83 Don't rinse fruit and vegetables under a running tap. Use a half-filled sink or bowl. This water can then be reused on your garden or plants.

84 Don't put frozen food under a running tap to defrost it. Plan ahead and put it in the refrigerator to defrost or use the microwave.

85 Only use pans and cookware that are an appropriate size. A large saucepan for a small quantity of food means you'll waste energy, as well as the excess water.

86 Use only enough water to cover vegetables when boiling them. Your food will cook faster.

87 Keep the lid on saucepans when boiling food. The water will boil faster and less will be lost to evaporation. That way you won't have to top up saucepans if the water boils low.

DID YOU KNOW?

A kitchen tap uses around 15–20 litres a minute.

88 Keep the water you've used to boil your vegetables in. It can be stored in the fridge or freezer and reused in soup or to cook more vegetables. Alternatively, wait for it to cool down and use it on your plants.

89 Steaming vegetables is a much more water-efficient and healthy way to cook them. Steaming uses less water and means that fewer nutrients are lost in the cooking process.

90 Microwaving vegetables uses no water at all and still retains most of the nutrients.

91 Just fill the kettle with as much water as you need. Use the cup you'll be drinking from to fill it. This will save water and energy.

General

92 Ensure all taps both inside and in the garden are always turned off tightly so they don't drip. However, don't force taps, as you can damage them and actually cause leaks.

> **DID YOU KNOW?**
>
> A dripping tap can waste up to anywhere from 30 to 200 litres a day. That's over 70,000 litres a year!

93 Develop a regular routine of checking all indoor and outdoor taps, washers and pipes for leaks, cracks and breaks, as well as checking all appliances in the house that use water.

94 Learn how to repair leaking taps. A new washer is cheap and easily available at hardware stores, as well as being simple to replace.

95 Ensure that everyone in your household know the location of your property's shut-off tap, and how to turn it off. If a pipe bursts, this can not only save litres of water, but also extensive property damage.

96 Check that the threads and handles of all taps both inside and outside are not clogged up with dirt, mould or other substances. This gunk can make it hard to turn the tap off completely, meaning there's more chance the tap will drip.

97 Your hot water system can develop leaks and drips. Regularly check all pipes and pressure valves to ensure this often hidden-away device isn't a silent water waster.

98 Hot water pipes can be insulated to prevent heat loss, meaning you won't have to run the water while you wait for it to heat up.

99 The tank of your hot water system can also be insulated to prevent the water cooling down as it is stored. Check with a plumber or your water supplier, and ensure that you're not covering the thermostat or any outlets or furnaces if you use gas hot water.

100 Reduce the flow of water through your taps by installing water pressure reduction devices in your pipes and taps. Less pressure means less water comes through. Talk to a licensed plumber about other ways you can reduce water pressure.

101 A lot of water is wasted by running extra cold water to cool down extremely hot water. Set the temperature on your hot water system at a reasonable temperature and save that extra water.

102 Don't send water from flower vases down the drain – use it to water pot plants or the garden.

103 Use the old water from your pet's drinking bowl to water pot plants or the garden instead of throwing it away.

104 When constructing paths and patios, use porous materials that allow water to soak through.

105 Design patio areas, courtyards and walkways so that any run-off water flows to lawns or garden beds.

106 Don't buy your children water toys that require a steady supply of water from the tap or need constant refilling to operate.

107 Always think before pouring excess water down the drain. It can always be used for watering or cleaning.

108 Ensure all fountains, ponds or water features use pumps that recycle the water.

109 Watch out for water wastage in your neighbourhood. Report broken pipes or hydrants, as well as water wasters!

110 Leftover ice in cups from takeaway outlets can be put on pot plants or the garden, instead of discarded.

111 Use disposable nappies instead of cloth ones and drastically reduce water usage in your washing machine. Investigate nappy recycling services so your used nappies don't harm the environment.

DID YOU KNOW?

Hosing down concrete wastes up to 1,000 litres an hour.

Cleaning

112 Don't water your concrete - you won't grow anything! Never use a hose to clean your driveway or footpath. Use a rake or a broom and pop the sweepings on the compost heap.

113 Use liquid cleaning products when you clean the bathroom. Use water only when you're ready to rinse.

114 Fill a bucket and use that to rinse your bathroom after cleaning. This will uses a lot less water than running the tap or shower.

115 Each time you clean out your fish tank, use the old water to water the garden. This water is rich in nitrogen and phosphorous, making it an excellent fertiliser.

116 When your pets need a bath, wash them outside in the garden on lawns or ground cover that needs watering. Make sure the detergent you use is suitable for your plants or grass.

117 Don't wash pets using a hose. Instead, fill a bucket or use a hose with a nozzle that can be shut off when not in use.

Washing the car

118 Put the environment ahead of a shiny car! Only wash your car when it is absolutely necessary.

119 Next time you wash your car, park it on the lawn instead of in the driveway or street. This way, your lawn will get watered at the same time. Alternatively, park it somewhere where the water will flow to the lawn or a garden bed.

120 Don't keep the hose running while you wash the car. Use a light spray and only use it at the start and end of the wash.

121 Use a hose with a nozzle that you can turn off. That way you won't have to keep the water running while you walk back to the tap to turn it off.

DID YOU KNOW?

Washing the car with the hose running can waste anywhere from 50–300 litres of water.

122 A bucket of water can do just as good a job as a hose and uses much less water.

123 Instead of wetting and rinsing the whole car at once, wet and wash the car in small sections, using a bucket to reduce water usage.

124 Don't use a water-hungry high-pressure cleaning device to wash your car.

125 Use a commercial car wash. If the business recycles all the water it uses, it will waste less water than washing the car at home.

126 Investigate products that clean and polish the car without using any water. Car washing wipes and sprays are becoming increasingly available.

127 Get up early on cold, dewy mornings and use that layer of dew on your car to wipe it down. This will reduce the number of times you'll need to wash your car.

Swimming pool

128 Make sure you cover your swimming pool or spa with a well-fitting pool cover or blanket. This will greatly reduce evaporation, saving water, but also heating bills and chemicals.

129 Check that your pool cover still easily allows rainwater into the pool, meaning you won't have to fill it as often.

130 Be especially vigilant about covering your pool on windy days. More wind means more evaporation. Try to discourage use of the pool on windy days.

DID YOU KNOW?

Evaporation from an uncovered swimming pool can waste up to 200 litres a day.

131 Install a windbreak to reduce evaporation caused by the wind. A windbreak could be a hedge, a screen or a fence.

132 Inspect your pool regularly for leaks and make sure any leaks are repaired quickly.

DID YOU KNOW?

Evaporation from an uncovered pool over the course of a year can equal the entire volume of the pool.

133 Turn down the temperature on heated pools and spas. Warmer water will evaporate much quicker than cooler water.

134 Turn off any pool fountains, waterfalls, sprays or water slides. Sprayed water will evaporate faster than still water.

135 Keep water levels lower to prevent water splashing over the sides. However, ensure the level is still suitable for your filtration equipment.

136 Encourage pool users to stop splashing and water fights. This will decrease the amount of water that gets splashed over the side.

137 Check the weather forecast before topping up or refilling your pool. A rainy day will fill the pool naturally without wasting tap water.

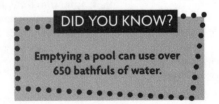

DID YOU KNOW?

Emptying a pool can use over 650 bathfuls of water.

138 Don't use a pool cleaning machine that sprays the tiles. Water will be wasted through evaporation or lost over the side of the pool.

139 Use a pool cleaning machine that recycles and reuses the water as it cleans.

140 Ensure your pool stays clean and well maintained. This will reduce the chance that you will have to drain it due to algae or poor water quality.

141 Some people empty their pools in winter. You should only drain your pool when absolutely necessary. This should only be necessary if water quality is an issue or the pool has a leak.

142 When refilling a pool, keep a close watch on the water level so you don't over-fill. Don't just pop the hose in and walk away. An unsupervised hose can waste litres of water.

DID YOU KNOW?

It can take up to 100,000 litres to fill a swimming pool.

143 Regularly check your pool's chemical balance. This way you won't need to top it up with more water to dilute down chemicals or, worse, completely refill it.

144 In extreme drought conditions, you may be restricted from refilling the pool. If your pool becomes unusable, water in the pool can be used on your garden. Ensure the chlorine levels are safe for your plants. Use a bucket to transport water and keep the cover on the pool during this period so water isn't lost due to evaporation, and you'll have more to use on your garden.

145 Instead of backwashing your filter to clean away collected refuse, if possible, clean it by hand. You'll save water and do a better job!

146 Install a cartridge filter, which can be manually washed down, instead of a sand filter, which requires backwashing.

DID YOU KNOW?

Backwashing a pool can use anywhere from 1000–4500 litres of water.

147 Check with a pool expert how frequently you should backwash your pool. Many people backwash their pool filters more often than needed, wasting water.

148 If possible, backwash the filter after rain. The pool will be fuller and will require less topping up, if at all.

149 Use piping to divert a nearby downpipe so that the rainwater from your roof and gutter flow into your swimming pool, keeping it topped up and reducing your reliance on mains water to fill the pool. Make the piping flexible enough to be removed once the pool is full and instead capture the water for your garden.

150 Alternatively, place tubs or buckets under downpipe outlets and capture the rainwater. Use this to top up the pool and keep some covered in reserve to refill after backwashing.

151 Plug the overflow line when the pool is in use and always when adding water. Keep the pool water in the pool.

152 Regularly check and maintain solar water heaters to ensure they don't leak or drip.

153 Roots from nearby plants and trees can damage pools, causing leaks. Make sure you don't place large trees too close to your pool, and check that the roots of your neighbours' plants aren't growing nearby either.

154 Some people reduce the numbers of showers they take in summer by regularly swimming in their pool, especially after exercise or before bed.

155 In extreme drought conditions, pool water can be used for cleaning, washing and flushing the toilet.

Coolers

156 Evaporative coolers use water by drawing air through a wet pad to cool it down. If you use a cooler with a two-speed fan, you use less water and energy running it at the lower speed.

157 Some coolers come with a thermostat sensor that will ensure your cooler will only run when the temperature reaches a certain level, saving you from running it unnecessarily and wasting water.

158 Regularly check and service evaporative coolers to ensure they are not leaking and are using water efficiently.

DID YOU KNOW?

If your cooler is using more than 6–8 litres of water an hour, there may be something wrong with it.

159 You'll use a lot less water if you only use your evaporative cooler when the temperature reaches 30°C.

160 A cooler is more efficient if you turn on the pump for a few minutes, soaking the pads, before you use the fan.

161 Choose a cooler that recirculates the water in the unit, instead of bleeding it all off after one use.

162 Check that your cooling is not bleeding off excessive amounts of water. Clamps that can be placed on the bleed line reduce the amount of water that is drained away.

163 Try using your cooler fan without the water pump, moving air around the room but not using any water.

164 Capture bled-off water from evaporative coolers and air conditioners into a container to water your plants

165 Alternatively, set up a system that will pipe bled-off water directly to your garden.

General

166 Don't water your garden in the heat of the day, as a great deal of water is lost to evaporation. On extremely hot days, watering during the day can even burn and damage plants and lawns. The best time to water is in the early morning or the late evening. Your garden will get a better drink and you won't find yourself replacing evaporated water. Morning is preferable, as there's less chance the water will sit on plants, leading to mildew and funguses.

167 Don't water your garden every day. It's much better for plants and lawns to receive a good soaking twice a week instead of a little bit of water every day. This will encourage the roots to grow deeper, resulting in hardier plants and a stronger root system that can better survive dry periods.

168 Water according to your garden's seasonal requirements. Your plants' watering needs will change over the year. In summer or hot weather, you may find that you need to water two or three times a week, whereas you may only need to water once a week in spring and autumn and not at all in winter or during a cold spell.

169 Don't assume your garden needs watering. Be sure to check whether it needs water before turning on the hose. Don't just examine plants – check the soil to see whether it is dry.

170 Know the watering needs of your plants. More plants die from over-watering than lack of water. Don't drown your plants.

171 Test soil moisture using a screwdriver or soil probe. Push it into the soil. Only water if it comes out dry or is difficult to push into the soil. If you can push it in easily, the soil is still holding enough water.

172 Water will absorb into the soil better if you water for several short periods instead of one long soaking. This will also prevent water run-off and waste. For example, water for 15 minutes or until puddles start forming and water starts running off. Let the water absorb for 20–30 minutes and then water for another 15 minutes.

173 Get to know how well your garden absorbs water. Water for 15 minutes, let it soak in for 20 minutes and then test to see how deeply it has absorbed. Dig a small hole where you've watered to see how far down the water has soaked. The top 15–20 cm should be damp.

174 Don't allow more than a centimetre of water to collect on the soil. This excess water can easily run off and be wasted. Only water as quickly as the water is absorbed into the soil.

175 Ensure that your soil retains at least some moisture. If the soil dries out completely, it greatly reduces its capacity to absorb water. You'll need more water than you'd otherwise have used just to loosen the soil and get it moist again.

176 Divide your garden into several sections and only water one section at a time every couple of days. You'll use less water and develop plants that are hardier and more able to survive dry conditions.

177 Only water for short periods if your garden is on a slope, as it is harder for water to soak in and it runs off much easier. Give water time to soak in before watering again.

178 Watering on windy days wastes a lot of water, especially with sprinkler systems and fine sprays. Gusty winds can blow the water away from where it is intended, meaning more is needed to adequately water the garden. Wind also increases evaporation, meaning more water is needed to absorb deeply to plant roots.

179 Your garden won't need watering for 1-2 weeks after a good, soaking rain.

180 Use a rain gauge in your garden. It's not always obvious that rain has fallen overnight. Check the rain gauge before watering as the garden may not need it.

181 Check the four-day weather forecast for rain before watering. Your garden can hold out for a couple of days if rain is on the way.

182 Get to know what type of soil you have and what its water requirements are. Clay soil takes longer to absorb water but holds it longer, meaning you should water slowly in small amounts, such as with a drip system. Loam can absorb water faster and needs moderate watering. Sandy soil drains and dries out faster, meaning it needs small amounts of water more frequently.

183 Improve the water absorption of clay soils by digging in liquid or powdered gypsum.

184 Understand what sort of plants will grow best in your soil type. Plants that have adapted to different soils will need less watering.

185 Regularly digging, hoeing or tilling the soil will help loosen and aerate it, meaning that water can penetrate to the roots much better. This is especially useful in summer when the soil can become baked hard in the heat.

186 Start a compost heap and dig it into your soil, especially before planting new beds or lawns. Water-holding organic matter will help aerate and keep moisture in the soil. Use leaves, garden rubbish, lawn clippings, food scraps, manure, sawdust, wood chips, untreated shredded paper, vacuum cleaner refuse and even hair in your compost heap.

187 Mix in water crystals with your compost when you dig near your plants' roots. Water crystals are made of a polymer material and can absorb up to 500 times their weight in water. They increase the water-holding capacity of soil and absorb excess water, preventing run-off. They keep soil moist and provide a reservoir of water for thirsty plants during dry spells.

188 Regularly weed your garden and lawn. Water-hungry weeds compete with your plants and grass for water, meaning your garden needs more water to survive.

189 Only fertilise your lawn and garden lightly and only if necessary. Fertiliser increases plants' need for water. An organic fertiliser is the best choice.

190 Use a soil wetting agent to make the soil less water repellent, or hydrophobic. Soil wetting agents prevent water from beading on the surface and running off, and make the soil more absorbent.

191 Collect rainwater from downpipes and use it to water your garden. It can be as simple as a cheap plastic bucket or as elaborate as a rainwater tank system.

192 Alternatively, use pipes and hoses to move water directly from your downpipes to garden beds and trees.

DID YOU KNOW?

Forgetting to turn off a sprinkler can waste 1000 litres of water an hour.

193 Reuse your washing-up water from the kitchen on the garden. Dishwater is actually good for keeping aphids away.

194 When using a hose or sprinkler, set an alarm or kitchen timer. That way time won't get away from you and you'll be aware of how long you've been running a sprinkler or watering the garden.

195 Should drought and water restrictions prevent the use of hoses and sprinklers and limit the amount of water you can use, look at how you can best use your available ration of water. Reuse whatever household water you can and prioritise your plants on their water needs. Focus on saving established plants such as trees and shrubs. Use your available tap water on plants that will be hard to replace or have taken a long time to mature and will die without water. Use greywater on plants that require only a little water to survive and newer, less established plants. Don't waste water on low-value plants and annuals. If necessary, discuss your plants water needs with a local nursery. Some plants might not need watering at all and will recover even after completely drying out.

196 Have a reasonable expectation of how your garden will look in the summer. It is unrealistic to think your garden and lawn will be green and lush during a long, dry spell. Do your best to help your plants through the summer but don't worry about plants that can be replaced and remember that most lawns will bounce back.

Design

197 A well-designed garden can be one of the biggest water savers for your household. Use Xeriscape™ ('xero' meaning dry and 'scape' from landscape) principles to create and maintain your garden. Xeriscaping focuses on creating lush, cleverly designed gardens that don't need a lot of water. The main principles of this form of gardening include good garden planning and design, soil preparation, careful plant selection, practical lawn areas, smart irrigation, mulching and ongoing maintenance.

198 If you understand your garden and design according to its features, you can drastically reduce its water requirements. Look at what areas get the most sun, frost, shade and wind. Think about how slopes can be used and know your soil type and what the drainage is like. Plan how you want to use your garden and how much time you want to spend maintaining it.

199 Plant drought-resistant species with low water requirements. Water-wise plants include cacti and succulents, but there are many other plants that don't need a lot of water. Look for plants with small, hairy, waxy, leathery or needle-shaped leaves. Plants with grey leaves, lighter undersides of leaves and leaves that close are also good choices. Speak to your local nursery for expert advice.

200 Choose native plants, especially ones from your local area. Local plants may be able to survive without any watering at all, as they have adapted to the rain levels of your area. Natives also need less fertilising and encourage native birds to visit your garden.

201 Choose exotic plants from other parts of the world with a similar climate to your own. Plants from the Mediterranean, South America, Africa and North America can be appropriate choices.

202 Group plants with similar water needs together. This is known as hydrozoning and is a useful water saving tool. Place plants with higher water needs together, and you'll only have to run one sprinkler. This system also lets you take advantage of different microclimates in your garden. For example, some plants will thrive in the cooler, shaded area under the eaves, while others will prefer to be at the top of a slope where they are exposed to the elements and get the afternoon sun.

203 Don't plant new garden beds or lawns in the summer. New plants require a lot of water. Wait until autumn or winter, when it's more likely to be cooler and to rain. The plants will also have more time to become established before summer hits and will need less water in the heat.

204 Use large water-friendly groundcover plants across garden beds and on slopes to help prevent evaporation and retain water. Covering large areas with these hardy plants will protect the roots of other plants and keep the ground cool.

205 Alternatively, use lots of plants and trees to cover all the soil with a leafy canopy and create a shaded, cool garden. This will reduce evaporation and the soil will stay damp for a lot longer.

206 If you are planting species that need a lot of water, try and place them in cool areas where water naturally drains to, such as at the bottom of slopes and in watercourses.

207 Before you plant, install drains and channels near paved and concrete areas to collect run-off. Feed the outlets into garden beds.

208 Ask your local nursery about suitable plants to edge garden beds and lawns. These will stop soil erosion and water run-off, reducing watering needs.

209 Use mulch, rocks or bark to prevent water running off your garden on to driveways and footpaths. Cover an area about 20 cm wide alongside concrete areas and stop water going down the drain.

210 Use plants as screens and windbreaks to protect your garden from hot winds that speed up evaporation, dry out soil, reduce moisture and prevent sprinklers from working efficiently.

211 Include feature walls, shadecloth and screens in your garden design to increase shade, cool your garden and reduce plants' exposure to wind.

212 Use climbing plants on fences and pergolas to cool the garden and provide shade in summer. A deciduous plant will lose its leaves in the winter, letting the sun through.

213 It is possible to have a water feature that doesn't waste water. Position it in a shady, screened area to reduce evaporation and use recycled water if possible. If the feature has moving water, use a pump that recirculates the water. Fountains or waterfalls that trickle or cascade slowly or produce large droplets means water evaporates slower than features that spray water in the air, splash, produce a mist or use fast-moving, high-pressure movements. Deeper and smaller features will lose less water to evaporation than wider and shallower ones. Remember to turn off any pumps when not needed, and try not to run fountains in the heat of the day.

Lawn

214 Reduce the amount of lawn areas in your garden. Lawns are the biggest water-consumers in your garden and are also high maintenance.

Keep lawn for areas where it's necessary for the function of your garden. Plant native and water-friendly trees and grasses in unused lawn areas.

215 A good groundcover is a more water-friendly option than turf. Groundcovers reduce evaporation and need less watering. Make a path or walkway through groundcovers using pavers, stepping stones or sleepers.

216 Don't use lawn for walkways and high-traffic areas. Replace grass with pavers, courtyards, decks and patios.

217 Hard-wearing paving, gravel or pebbles are better options than grass for areas used for parking the car, hanging out the laundry and barbecuing.

218 If you can't live without a lawn, speak to your nursery about the best grasses to use for your region and climate, and how you use your garden. Native grasses are more drought tolerant and require less water.

219 If possible, place lawns in lightly shaded areas. This will reduce evaporation and will also be nice and cool.

220 Use soft artificial turf under children's play equipment. Grass will wear away in these high-use areas, and artificial grass is just as safe and doesn't need watering.

221 Get rid of lawn in your front garden and replace it with screening plants. As well as using less water, this will also reduce street noise and serve as a fence, giving you more privacy.

222 Replace grass with river pebbles and succulents to create a low-maintenance, no-water garden.

223 Keep lawn areas as level as possible to allow water to be absorbed quickly with minimal runoff.

224 Don't plant lawns on slopes. These areas don't retain water well and are also hard to maintain and mow.

DID YOU KNOW?

Up to 90% of water used in the garden is spent on the lawn.

225 Don't plant grass in thin strips or small areas along paths or driveways. These areas dry out faster and you'll find a lot of the water will be wasted on the concrete surface.

226 Dig your soil to a depth of at least 15 cm and add compost before planting a lawn. If the soil is loose and well aerated, you'll grow a healthier, less water-hungry lawn.

227 Raise the blade on your lawn mower, especially in summer. Try and keep the grass at least 2–3 cm long. Long grass grows deeper roots, which allows the soil to hold water better. It also shades the soil, preventing water evaporation and reducing the chance of your grass getting burnt.

228 Don't mow your lawn on extremely hot days. Baking sun can stress and burn lawns, and the shorter grass will allow for more evaporation.

229 Grasscycle and improve your lawn! Take the catcher off your mower and leave the grass clippings on the lawn. This will protect the lawn from evaporation and also provide nutrient-rich fertiliser. Grass is mostly made up of water and will decompose into the soil quickly. Grasscycling won't cause thatching. Mow frequently so that only small clippings are produced and break up large clumps with a mower or a rake. Some mowers will even mulch the clippings and force them into the soil as you mow.

230 Plant lawns separately from garden beds instead of integrating them. Lawns require more water than other plants and are best watered with a sprinkler. If you do have small patches of lawn, water them by hand so you're not unnecessarily wasting water by using a sprinkler on plants that don't need them.

231 Soak lawns every few days instead of a small amount every day. Small amounts of water are more likely to evaporate before penetrating the soil. You'll also help your lawn become more drought resistant and develop a strong root system.

232 Before you water your lawn, check to see if it needs it. If the grass springs back after you step on it, it won't need any more water. Only water if the grass remains flat after you step on it.

233 In severe drought conditions, you can stop watering and allow your lawn to dry out and turn brown. Grass will regenerate quickly after rain. Just ensure you keep traffic on your lawn to a minimum.

234 Don't over-water your lawn. Place a bucket or container on your lawn and turn off your sprinkler when 1 cm of water collects in the bottom.

235 Experiment with your watering to find out how much water your lawn really needs. Over several weeks, gradually reduce the amount of water used or the length of time spent watering. When there's an obvious effect on the grass, you'll know to slightly increase your watering to the right level.

236 Use the dew of cool mornings to water your lawn. To stop dew evaporating, drag a hose or run a broom across your grass. This will help the water move from the blades to the soil.

237 Water reaches the roots much easier if you aerate your lawn. Drive small holes in your lawn about 15 cm apart. You can leave the holes empty or fill them with sand - the water will reach the roots where it's needed and there's also less chance of run-off.

238 Areas that dry out easily such as near paths, driveways and paving especially benefit from aeration. Use a root feeder probe to get water directly to these areas without water running off.

239 Aerate and de-thatch lawns in spring and late summer. De-thatching removes clumps of grass that prevent water reaching the roots. De-thatching allows water to penetrate the soil faster and helps the roots grow stronger.

240 When children want to play under the sprinkler on hot days, try and place it in shaded areas where water won't evaporate as quickly. Choose an area that needs water the most. Remember not to rewater that part of the lawn later on.

Trees and garden beds

241 Using mulch on garden beds is one of the best ways to reduce water usage in your garden. Mulch helps the soil retain moisture, reduces evaporation and run-off, keeps soil cool, prevents erosion and suppresses weed growth. Organic material, such as bark, wood chips, straw and leaves, works better, but inorganic material, such as rocks, pebbles, river stones and gravel, will still reduce your water usage. Spread mulch to a depth of 50–100 mm on garden

beds, but keep it a few centimetres away
from plant stems and bases to avoid rot
and fungus. Never use plastic sheeting
under mulch.

242 Remember to
top up the mulch
in your garden at
the start of every
spring. This will
prevent the soil
drying out as
the weather gets
hotter, requiring
more water to
moisten it.

DID YOU KNOW?

Using mulch on your garden
can reduce evaporation by
up to 75%.

243 When watering, make sure the water
falls on the roots, not the leaves.
Water that falls at the base of plants
will soak in and go straight to where
it's needed, whereas water that falls on
leaves is wasted through evaporation.

244 Individually water new plants
instead of using a watering system.
These plants require water more often
but in smaller amounts.

245 When you plant your garden, dig a wide but shallow hole two or three times wider than the pot or root bag. This makes a wider water basin for your plant's roots. This encourages water penetration.

246 When planting garden beds, ensure that they are level or slope inwards to stop water running off.

247 You can also make raised, inward-sloping basins or trenches around the stems and trunks of individual plants. This will reduce run-off and improve water absorption.

248 Only use sprinklers for lawns. Using a bucket, watering can or hose to individually water plants and trees gives more control over how much water is used and allows you to tailor your watering to each plant's needs.

249 Don't remove shading branches from trees. The shade keeps the roots and soil cool and reduces evaporation, and your garden will benefit from the leaves and litter that accumulate on the soil.

250 Use root feeders and aerators to get water straight to the roots of your plants and trees with no evaporation. Insert the feeders about 40 cm deep for large trees and 20–30 cm for garden beds, bushes and smaller trees.

251 Make your own root watering system using a plastic drink bottle. Make small holes in the base of the bottle and bury it upright in your garden beds or next to a tree, leaving the bottle neck sticking out. Fill the bottle with water and don't forget to screw on the lid to prevent evaporation. The water slowly seeps out of the holes into the root area and the ground will stay moist. Check the bottle's water level using a dry stick and refill when necessary.

252 Insert a length of pipe or tubing into the ground next to trees and plants. Watering through the tube will get water straight to the roots.

253 Established, healthy trees can usually survive drought with little or no water, especially if they provide a lot of shade over their root area.

254 Deciduous trees are dormant in the winter and may not need watering at all.

255 Check where pipes and sewers run through your property before planting large trees. The roots of these trees can break pipes in their search for water. Be careful not to plant too close to your house and its plumbing system.

DID YOU KNOW?

The following trees have large, vigorous root systems that can damage pipes. Try to avoid planting these trees near sewerage and water pipes.

- Apple
- Ash
- Birch
- Box elder
- Broad-leaved and prickly paperbarks
- Casuarina species (river oaks, she oaks)
- Cottonwood
- Elm
- Figs and ficus
- Honeysuckle
- Jacaranda
- Large eucalypt trees
- Lilac
- Maple
- Norfolk pines
- Oak
- Pepper tree
- Plane
- Poplars
- Russian olive
- Silky oak
- Sycamore
- Umbrella tree
- Willows

Watering systems

256 Ensure all taps, hoses, sprinklers and irrigation systems and their fittings do not leak, and immediately repair or replace any that do. Use hose washers to prevent leaks.

257 Check sprinkler and drip heads have not become clogged or blocked with mud or refuse, increasing the risk of hoses bursting or cracking under the higher pressure.

258 Planting your garden in zones according to water use means you can plan your irrigation system to match the water needs of each zone. If you have an automatic system, use separate timers or a multi-timer for each zone so you can schedule waterings appropriately.

259 Consider banning hosepipes from your garden and use a watering can or bucket to water your plants. You'll be more accurate with your watering.

260 Use hoses with a shut-off nozzle so you can stop the flow of water when it isn't needed.

261 Make sure children know not to play with hoses, sprinklers and taps in the garden.

262 Use sprinklers that spray large droplets close to the ground instead of a fine mist. This will reduce the amount of water lost to wind drift.

263 Run sprinklers at as low a water pressure as possible, preventing wind drift and over-spraying. This way you won't water the garden faster than the soil can absorb it.

264 Place sprinklers as far from paving, footpaths and driveways as possible. Face them towards garden beds to reduce the chance of water being lost down the drain.

265 Find out what water pressure your sprinkler best operates at. This will improve your sprinkler's water efficiency.

266 Don't leave hoses and sprinklers unattended. That way you can monitor how well water is absorbing and how much water is running off. There's also less chance you'll forget they're running.

267 To ensure sprinklers sufficiently cover an area, know the best location for them. You won't have to move them or run them as frequently.

268 Use a container or rain gauge when you run your sprinkler and time how long it takes to fill to the equivalent of 10 mm of rain.

269 Only use sprinklers on lawns. Instead of using sprinklers and misters on garden beds, trees, ground cover and planters use a drip system to water. Drip systems use flow-control devices or emitters to slowly drip water directly to the root area of plants. This uses a lot less water, increases absorption into the soil, stops wind drift and lowers run-off and evaporation rates. Drip systems are particularly effective for slopes.

DID YOU KNOW?

A dripper can use as little as 2–8 litres of water an hour.

270 Speak to an irrigation specialist to find out if sub-surface watering systems are suitable for your garden. These sit under the ground and release water directly to the roots. There's almost no evaporation or run-off with this kind of system.

271 If you can't afford the time to monitor a sprinkler, install a tap timer that you manually set the time for whenever you water.

272 If you're using an automatic timer, regularly watch your watering system run through a full cycle. Make sure water is not running off and being wasted

DID YOU KNOW?

An improperly maintained automatic sprinkler can use over 50,000 litres per year. A regular sprinkler running for the same amount of time uses about 25,000 litres.

and adjust the system until all water is absorbed.

273 Adjust your automatic timer over the course of the year as the weather changes.

274 Use an automatic system with a rain, humidity and moisture sensor that shuts off when it is not needed. That way you won't end up watering the garden while it is raining, or flooding already moist soil.

275 The best way to use your controller is the same as the best way to water lawns and gardens. Program it to run a few days apart. When you do run it, program several cycles with a break between each cycle. For example, instead of watering for 15 minutes, run your system for 5 minutes at a time, with 15 minutes between each watering. This allows water to deeply absorb into the soil and promotes strong root systems.

> ## DID YOU KNOW?
>
> **Automatic irrigation systems often do not save any water at all because the owners don't monitor the system for weather and seasonal variations.**

276 Ensure you reprogram your timer if you live in an area where water restrictions mean you can only water on set days. Alternatively, turn off your timer and water by hand.

Pot plants and hanging baskets

277 Plants in containers need to be watered more often that those in garden beds, however make sure you don't over-water your pot plants.

278 Use pots and containers that aren't porous. Plastic pots won't allow water to seep through.

279 If you're using terracotta pots, choose pots that are glazed or painted. Applying a sealant before you use an untreated terracotta pot will also reduce water seepage.

280 Alternatively, sit plastic pots inside decorative terracotta pots.

281 Use self-watering pots that trap excess water in a section that the plant can constantly drink from. There are even varieties available that allow you to pour water directly into the reservoir.

282 Use peat moss and water crystals in your potting mixture to aid water retention. Remember to replace water crystals every few years.

283 Mulch your pot plants to prevent evaporation and stop them drying out as quickly.

284 Grow a groundcover around the base of trees in large planters. You'll stop evaporation and aerate the soil.

285 Cover the soil of small pots with decorative pebbles. This works much the same way as mulch and looks very attractive.

286 Use saucers under potted plants so you can collect and use run-off water.

287 Raise your pots and planters to improve their drainage and collect the excess run-off in a container to reuse on your plants.

288 Don't leave pot plants and hanging baskets in areas that are always in the direct sun, especially during the middle of the day. Try to place pots in shaded areas.

289 Water two plants at once. Hang baskets above garden beds, lawns or pot plants so that run-off water is used for other plants instead of being wasted.

290 Purchase hanging baskets that have a tray or reservoir to save excess water that the plant can drink or that can be reused on other plants.

291 Water your pot plants by placing ice blocks in the soil or under the mulch. This slow-release form of watering helps prevent run-off and allows you to regulate the amount of water your plants use.

General

292 It can be easy to find out if you have a leak somewhere. Before you go to bed, turn off all taps and water appliances both inside and outside the house and record the reading on the water meter. Make sure no one uses any water overnight. When you get up in the morning, check to see if the reading has changed. If it has, it's likely you have a leak. You can also check the meter during the day – just make sure you don't use any water for at least three hours.

DID YOU KNOW?

A leaking pipe, tap or water appliance can be one of the biggest wasters of water in your household. Often people don't even know they have a leak.

293 A higher water bill than expected may be a sign that you have a leak. Regularly monitor your water bills and check for anomalies.

294 Don't make temporary repairs to leaks, such as wrapping pipes in duct tap. Often water will still seep through temporary repairs, wasting water. Leaks can become major breaks if not properly repaired.

295 Install a leak detection system. These devices usually operate via a water sensor that either sounds an alarm or automatically shuts down the system when it detects a leak. Leak detection systems can be used with individual appliances or monitor the whole house via a series of sensors that shut down the mains water supply if a leak occurs.

296 Learn how to change a leaking tap's washer and keep a supply of washers on hand. If you fix leaks as soon as you discover them, you'll reduce the amount of water wasted, and also your water bill.

297 Get a plumber to check your water pressure and your pipes. Pipes that are not adequate for the velocity and pressure of the water going through them can break and leak.

298 A leaking tap can be quite obvious but taps can leak in other places apart from the spout. Check under the sink or basin and watch to see if water is leaking out of the handles.

DID YOU KNOW?

Some of the most common household leaks include toilets that won't stop running, constantly dripping taps, appliances not properly connected to taps and pipes and leaking sprinkler systems.

299 If you can't readily locate a leak, it could be because your pipes are leaking in the walls or underground. Immediately contact an expert to investigate this further.

Bathroom fixtures

300 While leaking taps are usually obvious, you may not notice your bathtub or shower taps leaking, as water already collects in tubs or showers after bathing. Try drying the bottom of your shower or tub before you go to bed and check in the morning to see if the bottom is wet.

301 In hot weather, this method may not work if it is warm enough for drips to evaporate quickly. Instead, scatter some talc around the plug hole or under the tap outlet. If water has leaked overnight, the talc will be broken.

DID YOU KNOW?

How much water can a leaky tap waste?
60 drops a minute can add up to over 8,000 litres a year.
90 drops a minute can add up to over 12,000 litres a year.
120 drops a minute can add up to over 19,000 litres a year.

Toilets

302 Flush your toilet and wait for the bowl and cistern to fill up. If water won't stop running into the bowl or you can hear water running (often it's like a hissing sound), your toilet is leaking.

303 To check for a silent leak, place some bright food colouring in the cistern. Don't flush the toilet for 15–20 minutes and then check the water in the toilet bowl. If you have a silent leak in your cistern, the water in the bowl will now be coloured by the food dye.

304 If water won't stop running, check the floater inside your cistern. If you lift the arm and the water stops, the floater is faulty or the water level is set too high, meaning water is constantly running into the overflow outlet tube into the bowl.

305 Turn off the toilet tap and flush the toilet. When the cistern is empty, check the water inlet valve to ensure it is not damaged or worn, and replace it if it is, or contact a plumber.

306 Check that the flush ball or flapper fits the flush valve seat correctly. Straighten it if it is crooked and replace it if it wears out. Clean away scale or corrosion with a steel wool pad or sandpaper.

307 Check that the end of the refill tube is correctly placed above the water level.

Greywater systems

308 Because it doesn't use mains water, a leaking greywater system won't affect your water meter. Regularly check your greywater system for leaks. Look for water leakage and drips. If you have a leak, you may also be able to detect a musty, organic smell.

309 Check the ground around your greywater system for an underground leak. If the ground is spongy or gives off a musty, organic smell, do some careful exploratory digging to find the source of the leak. You may need to contact your greywater system supplier.

310 Check all pipes, taps and connections in your greywater system to confirm that none of them are leaking, and repair or replace any parts that do leak.

Hot water and plumbing systems

311 Check your hot water system regularly for leaks. Look for water under the tank to see if it is leaking – this is often quite obvious. Check for obvious splits and corrosion in the tank and also check the top of the tank to ensure it is not damaged.

312 Inspect all hot and cold pipes running in and out of your heater to ensure they are dry and not cracked.

DID YOU KNOW?

Fixing a leaking hot water system or tap won't just save you water – it will also save you gas or electricity.

313 If your tank is partially underground, you may need to do some careful digging to check for leaks. Spongy soil is often an indicator of a leak, however sandy soils can drain water away from the surface, so you may need to remind yourself to check around your tank at regular intervals. ⟫⟫⟫

314 Look for unexplained damp areas in the walls and floors of your house. These could be an indication of a leak in the water pipes. A foul odour or warm spots in the floor can also be signs of a leak.

315 If your home's foundations shift and crack or you find strange raised or sunken patches of earth in your garden, it can be a sign of a major water leak.

316 Walk around your garden and look for lawn areas that are greener or taller than the rest of the grass. Check for unexplained puddles and soggy spots.

Swimming pools

317 Get into a routine of checking your pool at regular intervals for leaks and cracks.

DID YOU KNOW?

Swimming pool leaks can cause major damage and waste enormous amounts of water. Even a minor leak can cause substantial wastage.

318 To establish if your pool is leaking, measure the water level in the pool and mark it with a pencil.

Your pool shouldn't lose more than 60 mm of water every 24 hours.

319 To check whether loss of water is evaporation or a leak, place a bucket on a step in the pool where the top half will be out of the water. Weight the bucket down and fill it with water to the same level as the pool. If in the pool water level is noticeably lower than the water level in the bucket after a day or so, it is likely you have a leak.

320 Check for damp soil around the pool and under your house. A leaking pool may also affect your neighbours' foundations as well.

321 Look for any cracks or gaps in the body of the pool and for any loose tiles.

322 If algae forms not long after you've chlorinated your pool, it may be a sign of a leak.

323 Cracks and breaks in decking, paving and concrete around your pool can be indicators of a leak.

DID YOU KNOW?

It is possible that as many as one in 20 swimming pools leaks.

324 If your pool subsides or settles into the ground, it is very likely that it is leaking.

325 See if you lose more water when the filter pump is running. Compare how much water you lose in a day when you run the filter with how much water you lose in a day without the filter. If you lose more with the filter, it may have a leak.

326 If you can't find a leak, call a pool specialist. Try and use a specialist that can detect a leak without you having to drain the pool. Many pool technicians can use equipment such as tiny cameras that can travel through pipes, highly sensitive microphones that listen for water or air escaping through cracks and compressed air pumps that force bubbles through breaks. A pool specialist can also use a coloured dye in the pool. By watching how the dye moves around the pool, they can establish whether a leak exists.

327 If you do have a leak, check that your pool repairer can fix the problem without having to drain the pool.

DID YOU KNOW?

A pool with a leak the size of a pin can lose up to 3,500 litres of water in 24 hours.

Watering systems and water features

328 To check for leaks in an underground watering system, cover all spray outlets, turn on the system and look for puddles forming on the surface. Examine your gutters and drains for excess water.

329 For above-ground systems, turn on the tap and walk the length of the hose or pipe check for water bubbling or spraying out.

330 Check all hose joints and pipe connections for leaks. These can usually be quickly mended by tightening the connection.

331 If water levels drop dramatically in water features, check the tubes, pipes and connections of any fountains or waterfalls. Inspect any ponds for leaks. You may need to do some careful exploratory digging around your feature. If you need to empty it to inspect it closely, reuse the water on your garden.

GREYWATER

RAINWATER HARVESTING

REBATES AND ASSISTANCE SCHEMES

Greywater systems

332 Water that goes down the drain, which has often been used only to rinse dishes or wash hands, goes directly into the sewerage system and, therefore, out into the ocean. Reusing your greywater will prevent this water from being wasted.

DID YOU KNOW?

Greywater is the term used to describe water that has already been used in the laundry, kitchen or bathroom. Water that has been used in flushing toilets is known as blackwater and is not suitable for use in greywater systems.

DID YOU KNOW?

Using greywater in the garden or to flush the toilet can help save up to 50 percent of the average household's fresh water consumption.

333 There are a range of greywater systems available, from very simple to quite complex, so carefully consider which one will suit your lifestyle before committing to anything. You won't use a system that doesn't suit your needs, and may ultimately waste more water than before.

334 Be sure to obtain approval to install a greywater system from your local council or water provider and ensure that a licensed plumber connects your greywater system to your plumbing. An incorrectly connected greywater system can leak and cause damage, and could even damage your mains plumbing system in extreme cases.

335 Use a greywater diverter to capture greywater from the washing machine, shower, laundry and bathroom taps to reuse on the garden. However, don't store greywater for long periods of time unless it is first treated.

336 Be very careful to ensure that the greywater system cannot interfere with the mains drinking water supply, as greywater contains organisms and bacteria which can be harmful if a person is directly exposed. A considerable amount of water is needed to flush out your drinking water pipes if they are contaminated.

337 Clean or replace the filter on your greywater system regularly to prevent leaks. However, don't use a hose to clean your filter – use a bucket filled with greywater.

338 Check with your local nursery to see whether the plants in your garden are suitable for the long-term use of greywater. Due to the detergents, nutrients and other matter contained in greywater, some of the more sensitive plants may be adversely affected. Don't waste greywater on these plants but save it for a more appropriate use. Choose detergents carefully to minimise the amount of pollution in your greywater. Non-phosphorous detergents are recommended.

339 Ensure that your greywater irrigation system is not over-watering your garden. While your plants need to get a sufficient amount of water, too much can cause deep percolation loss, which means that the water sinks too far below the ground for plant roots to reach it.

340 Invest in a greywater pre-treatment system and you'll be able to use greywater to flush your toilet and in the laundry.

Rainwater harvesting systems

341 Contact your local water supplier to enquire whether a rainwater tank in your area would be worthwhile and check with your local council to find out which, if any, permits will be required before you install your tank. Remember to seek the advice of a builder or engineer if you are planning on installing a large tank, to ensure that it is structurally sound. Ensure that your water tank is installed by a qualified professional, such as the tank manufacturer or a plumber. This will help to prevent mishaps during and after installation and make the system easier to maintain. It will also reduce the risk of cracks and leaks. Decide if you want to use your water for drinking, for household use such as washing and flushing the toilet or just on the garden.

DID YOU KNOW?

Rainwater harvesting is the term used to describe the collection of rainwater, generally from the roof of a house. Once the rain falls on the roof, it runs into the guttering system and into a downpipe which flows into a water-storage container. This container can be anything from a large pot or barrel to a rainwater tank connected to a plumbing system.

DID YOU KNOW?

If you use solely rainwater in your garden, you can reduce your household water use by 35–50%.

342 An integrated rainwater system can supply water for the whole house, meaning you won't need to use mains water at all. Some tanks have a monitor that will automatically switch your plumbing over to the mains supply if the rainwater tank runs out of water.

343 If you'd rather not use a water tank, you can still use a rainwater diverter to direct water from your downpipes through underwater pipes directly to your garden beds and trees, or into your swimming pool.

344 Check your roof for flashing, tar-based coatings and lead-based paint, as any of these things can make the water toxic. You could potentially have to throw away thousands litres of water if it is contaminated.

345 Clear out gutter systems regularly and keep all guttering and downpipes in a good state of repair. This will help to increase the effectiveness of your system, resulting in more water being harvested. Cover all gutters and openings in a fine mesh to keep out leaves, twigs and bugs.

346 Ensure that there are no tree branches hanging over the roof. Trees drop leaves which clog up the guttering, reducing the amount and quality of water you can harvest. Trees also encourage wildlife to live above your clean water catchment area, resulting in potential contamination from dung.

347 Fit a snug cover over your water tank to prevent evaporation. You'll have more water to use and also prevent insect contamination and unwanted animals or materials accessing your water.

348 Have a first flush diverter fitted to your system. This separates out the first quantity of water that drains off your roof, which contains most of the small insects and debris, and stops it from pouring into your tank, resulting in better quality water that can be used for household applications. Try and retain the initial quantity of dirtier water for use on your garden.

349 Fit a sump box to your system. This sits between the downpipe and the tank, slowing down the water flow in order to filter out any other residue and give you cleaner water for a wider range of uses.

>>>

350 Where possible, ensure that all pipes run downwards continuously so that water cannot sit stagnant in them between gushes. You won't waste water flushing out pipes or waiting for stagnant water to run through. Use gravity-fed pumps when possible, as these use less energy and are therefore less harmful to the environment.

351 Ensure that any excess water runs back into the stormwater pipe or an area of the garden that requires water rather than flowing down the drain.

352 Ensure that your water tank has sufficient aeration. Water that is not aerated may become stagnant and will need to be disposed of.

353 Fit a tap and hose to the side of your tank. You'll be more likely to use your rainwater if it is easily accessible. Make sure that you can connect an irrigation or sprinkler system to the tank.

354 Do not allow sediment to accumulate in your tank. Sediment build-up can contaminate your water, meaning you'll need to empty the tank and use a lot of water to flush it clean. Monitor sediment build-up and clean the inside of your tank at least every 2–3 years.

355 Be prepared for periods of low rainfall by making sure you always have some rainwater in reserve for your garden. If your tank becomes full, store the excess water in sealed watertight containers.

Rebate and assistance schemes

356 Contact your local water supplier and request a water audit of your home. In most states, this is provided free or at a discount price. The person who conducts the audit will highlight areas of your home where you can save water and may be able to offer information on possible rebates for any water-saving products you require.

DID YOU KNOW?

Rebate and assistance schemes for water-efficient appliances have been set up by most state and local governments and water providers to encourage people to reduce their household's fresh water consumption. These rebate and assistance schemes make the installation of water-saving appliances and devices more affordable. By taking advantage of them you can more easily contribute to protecting the environment and saving water.

359 A number of local water suppliers offer reduced-fee services where a licensed plumber will visit your home and fit new water-saving showerheads, water-flow regulators and even repair minor leaks. They will also provide you with further water-saving information.

357 Some state and local governments offer rebates on the cost of a water-wise garden assessment at your home.

358 Some state governments and water providers offer schemes that allow you to exchange old high-flow showerheads for water-saving low-flow ones at no charge.

360 You may be eligible for substantial rebates from state or local governments on the purchase and installation of a greywater or rainwater harvesting system.

361 Garden products such as wetting agents, water crystals and soil conditioners may be subject to rebate schemes.

362 AAA or WELS efficient showerheads, dual-flush toilets, tap timers and flow restrictors are some of the products that are included in various government rebate schemes.

363 Installing water-saving appliances such as WELS 4-star rated washing machines may make you eligible for government or council rebates.

364 Some state and local governments offer rebates on the purchase of pool covers.

365 Research the rebates available carefully, as you may be eligible for rebates from your state government in addition to those from your local government or water provider.

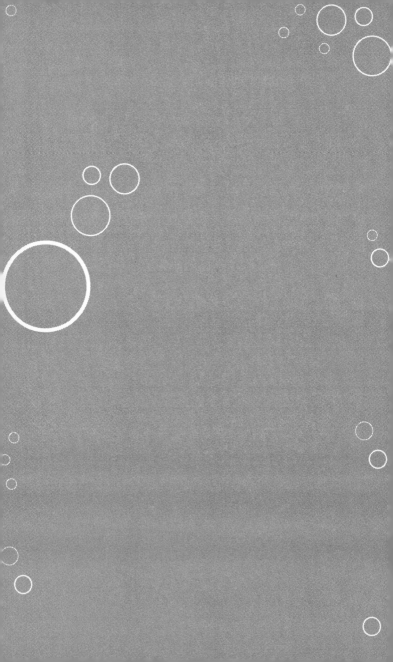

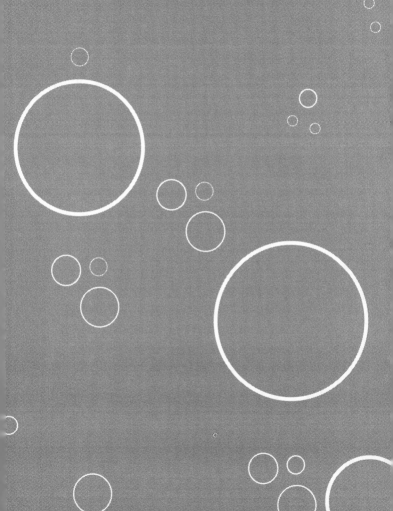

ACTIVITIES FOR KIDS

Water usage in your family

Who do you think the biggest water waster in your family is? **Does Mum wash her car with a bucket or a hose?** Does Dad let the water run when he's washing the dishes? **Do your brothers and sisters leave the tap running while they're cleaning their teeth?**

Ask everyone in your family to think about how they use water. How long do they spend in the shower, do they use the half-flush or full-flush buttons on the toilet and how do they brush their teeth?

Look at other areas of the house as well, such as how many times your washing machine and dishwasher are used every week, whether you use a sprinkler in your garden or if you have a pool that gets filled up often.

We use water in many parts of our lives. It's important that people use water carefully and don't waste it, or we might find it could run out.

1 Leaky taps

Dripping taps can waste a lot of water! It's easy to find out how much water a dripping tap wastes.

YOU WILL NEED:

- an unused sink
- an empty container with measurements marked on the side (some buckets have measurements on them)
- a watch or stopwatch
- a calculator

Follow these simple steps:

➡ Put the empty container under a tap that doesn't need to be used for an hour. Tell everyone in the house about your experiment so they don't interfere with it.

➡ Turn on the tap so that it is just slightly dripping.

➡ Record the time that the first drop of water falls into the container.

➡ In one hour, return to the sink and turn the tap off properly. Check the water level on the side of the container.

➡ Use a calculator to multiply the number of litres of water in the container by 24 (hours in a day). Next, multiply that number by 365 (days in a year). This will tell you how many litres of water is wasted by one dripping tap in a year. Now imagine if every house in Australia had a dripping tap!

Once you have done the experiment, don't forget to use the water from the container to water your garden!

Make a water map

YOU WILL NEED:
• paper • pens • coloured markers

Using water is so much a part of our everyday lives that we don't always realise when we are wasting it. To help make you and your family more aware of water usage, you can make a map of your home and the places in it that use water.

Follow these simple steps:

➡ Draw a map of your home. Don't forget to include the garden as well!

➡ Mark in all the different areas where water is used around the home by colouring the laundry, kitchen, bathroom, toilet and garden in different colours.

➡ Hang the picture up where that everyone in the house can see it. It should make them all start thinking about how much water they use!

It is important to recognise where water is being used so everyone can help to conserve it.

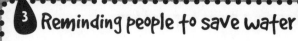

❸ Reminding people to save water

Not everyone knows how important saving water is for our environment. You can help other people become more aware of how important this is by making signs that you can hang up in your home.

YOU WILL NEED:
- paper
- coloured markers
- pencils
- tape or tack to hang the signs with

Follow these simple steps:

➡ Using the markers, write messages about saving water on the paper, such as 'Turn off the taps properly' or 'Don't spend too long in the shower'.

➡ Decorate your signs. You can draw pictures of people saving water!

➡ Hang the signs around the house near the areas they relate to, such as in the kitchen or bathroom.

Making these signs will remind your family and your guests that saving water is very important. People who are reminded about the water shortage are less likely to waste water.

4 Reading a water meter

The amount of water each house uses is measured by a water meter, which is usually found at the front of your property. While there may be different kinds of meters, they are all easy to read.

To read your water meter, first ask an adult where the one on your property is located. Once you have found it, remember these simple tips:

➡ A water meter is read from left to right.

➡ It has some numbers that are shaded and some that are not. The shaded areas represent litres and the non-shaded areas represent kilolitres.

➡ There are 1000 litres in a kilolitre.

If you look at a water meter while someone is having a shower, you should see it moving. Don't run the water just to see the meter move – that's a big water waster! Once you can read a water meter, you can then keep track of how much water your household is using.

5 Water survey

YOU WILL NEED:
• paper or a notebook
• a pen

Measuring how much water your household uses can be a huge help in saving water. To be able to complete this experiment you need to know how to read a water meter.

Follow these simple steps:

➡ Make a chart with each day of the week listed and space for a number. Record how much water your household uses daily by taking a reading of the water meter. Try and check the meter at the same time every day for a week.

➡ Add all of the readings up to get the total water use for the week.

➡ Take a reading every day over three or four weeks. Is the total the same each week?

➡ If there is a difference, think about why people have used more or less water. What reasons can you think of?

➡ Try to get everyone in your household to make a big effort to save water and see how much the reading has gone down after a week.

Knowing how much water your household uses really helps reduce water usage. Use what you have discovered to stop wasting water and use less water in your home.

Be a leak detective!

As you know, leaking taps can waste a lot of water. Help Mum and Dad by checking to see if there are any secret leaks around your home.

Follow these simple steps:

➜ After your family has finished using water in the evening, check the water meter and write down the reading.

➜ Make sure no one in the family uses water overnight. No late night toilet trips!

➜ When you get up in the morning, check the meter again.

➜ If the reading has changed, you may have a leak somewhere.

Remember, if someone has used a tap or the toilet during the night, it will have affected the reading.

7 Where does the rain go?

In Australia, the ground is very dry, which means a lot of our rainwater runs into gullies, streams, gutters and drains rather than soaking into the ground. You can see how much moisture the ground will absorb at your place.

YOU WILL NEED:
- several small, empty tin cans with the tops and bottoms removed (ask an adult to remove the ends as tin cans can be sharp)
- water
- a watch or stopwatch

Follow these simple steps:

→ Choose several different surfaces around your home. Some examples might be the front or back lawn, a garden bed, a sandpit, the driveway or a paved area.

→ Put a can on each of these surfaces. Push it into the ground slightly where possible.

→ Pour a third of a cup of water into each tin, one at a time, and record how long it takes for the water to be absorbed into the surface.

You'll see which areas of the environment are more likely to have water run off into rivers, gutters and drains, and which are more likely to absorb water and store it underground.

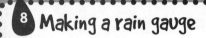

8 Making a rain gauge

Making a rain gauge can show you how much or how little rain is falling. The amount of rain we have determines how much water we have.

YOU WILL NEED:
- an empty jar
- a ruler
- sticky tape
- paper
- a pencil

Follow these simple steps:

➡ Tape the ruler to the side of the jar, ensuring that the 0 cm measurement is level with the bottom of the jar. This is now a simple rain gauge!

➡ Put the rain gauge outside in a clear space where it cannot catch drips from branches or gutters, or be knocked over.

➡ After a week, check your rain gauge. You can work out the average rainfall for that period by checking the level of the water against the ruler to see how many millimetres are in the jar. For instance, you may have had 5 millimetres of rainfall over that period.

Realising how little rain actually falls will help you understand how hard it is to replenish our water supply. It is much easier to save it than replace it.

9 Create a mini water cycle

All of the water on Earth has been here as long as the planet itself has been. Water never actually leaves the earth and no new water is ever introduced. The water on Earth goes through many different processes in many different forms in what is known as the 'water cycle'.

The water cycle begins with the sun warming the water in lakes, rivers and oceans until it turns into vapour and rises up into the air. This is called evaporation.

Once this water is in the air, it becomes colder and turns back into liquid and forms clouds. This is called condensation.

When the water in the clouds become too heavy to stay in the air, it falls to the ground as rain, hail or snow. This is called precipitation.

Some of the rain hits the Earth, soaks in and is stored underground. Some of it runs along the ground and flows back into lakes, rivers or the ocean. The process then starts all over again.

You can build your own mini water cycle, and observe the process yourself.

Follow these simple steps:

➨ Remove the lid from the jar and pour the rocks into the bottom.

➨ Pour the sand on top of the pebbles and the soil on top of the sand.

➨ Place the shell full of water on top of the soil to one side of the jar.

➨ Place the plant on top of the soil on the other side of the jar.

➨ Place the lid on the jar.

➨ Place the jar out in a sunny area.

YOU WILL NEED:
- a jar with a lid
- small rocks or pebbles
- sand
- soil
- a shell or other small container full of water
- a small, leafy plant

You should then be able to see the water cycle in action. Watch as the water condenses and reforms back into water droplets.

Understanding the water cycle will help you understand where our fresh water comes from.

10 Write a story

Imagine what it might be like if the city or town that you live in ran out of fresh water! Write a short story based on what you imagine. Read the story to your family and ask them to think about how we can save water.

11 Water police

Create a 'Water Police' badge for yourself and enforce the 'water laws' in your house!

YOU WILL NEED:
- cardboard
- a piece of paper
- coloured markers
- sticky tape
- a safety pin
- scissors
- a pen

Follow these simple steps:

➡ On the cardboard, draw the shape you want your badge to be and cut it out.

➡ Write 'WATER POLICE' on the badge and decorate it with the markers.

➡ With a small piece of sticky tape, stick the safety pin to the back of the badge.

➡ Write a list of water saving rules on the piece of paper with the pen.

➡ Wear your badge and enforce the water laws!

Keep reminding people about saving water and you'll find your family will use less water and save money on water bills.

12 Use the half flush!

Using the half-flush button on the toilet saves lots of water every day. People often forget to use it though! Create a sticker to place on or near your toilet reminding people to use the half-flush button all the time.

YOU WILL NEED:
- sticky label (large enough to write a message on)
- markers

Follow these simple steps:

➡ Write a reminder notice on the sticky label. The notice could read something like 'Use the half flush and save water!'.

➡ Decorate your stickers.

➡ Stick the label on or near the toilet where it is easily seen, but be careful to choose a surface that the sticker will not damage!

If you have more than one toilet, make as many stickers as you need!

13 Watering Fun

Watering the garden is fun! You can help your family water the lawn, and do it in a way that won't use much water.

YOU WILL NEED:
- hose
- outdoor tap
- sprinkler
- ruler
- plastic container, such as an ice cream container

Follow these simple steps:

➡ Make sure you do this activity in the cool of the evening or morning.

➡ Plug in the hose to the tap and attach it to the sprinkler. Put the sprinkler on the lawn in an area where it will get the grass wet but won't splash on to paving or driveways.

➡ Put the container on the lawn where it will get watered by the sprinkler.

➡ Record the time and then turn on the sprinkler.

➡ Check the water level in the container every few minutes with the ruler. When it reaches 1 cm, turn off the sprinkler and note how long the sprinkler was running. That's how long to run the sprinkler to give the lawn a good drink but not waste water!

Where does all the water go?

Make a list of the 10 ways that you think an average household uses the most water. Then search the internet to find out what the top 10 uses are. How closely did your list match? Did you find anything surprising?

Super shower saver!

Have a competition in your family to see who can use the least amount of water showering over a period of one week.

YOU WILL NEED:
- large piece of paper or cardboard
- coloured markers
- ruler

Follow these simple steps:

➡ Using the ruler, make a grid with 7 squares going across for each day of the week and as many squares down as there are people in your household.

➡ Write the days of the week across the top squares and your family members' names going down the side.

⟫⟫⟫

➡ Record how many showers each person has, and time them to see how long each person takes in the shower.

➡ At the end of the week, multiply how long each person takes in the shower by the amount of water your shower uses per minute. You can check this by running your shower for ten seconds and collecting the water in a bucket. Multiply this by 6 and that's how much water per minute your shower uses.

➡ Give the winner a small prize and see if everyone can do better next week

No one is allowed to skip a shower just to try and win!

16 Who needs water?

Create a poster, headed 'We Need Water'. On the poster, draw all of the things you can think of that need fresh water to survive.

YOUR OWN WATER SAVING IDEAS

YOUR OWN WATER SAVING IDEAS

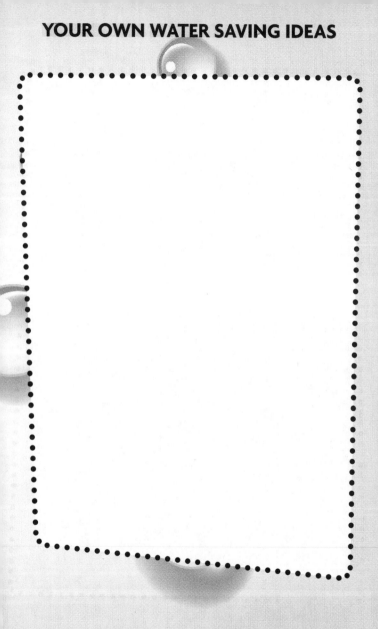

YOUR OWN WATER SAVING IDEAS

YOUR OWN WATER SAVING IDEAS

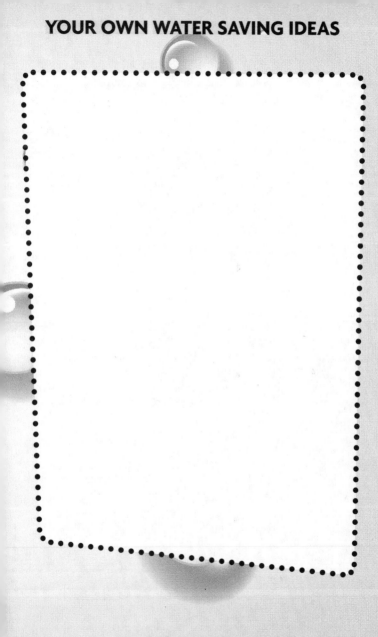

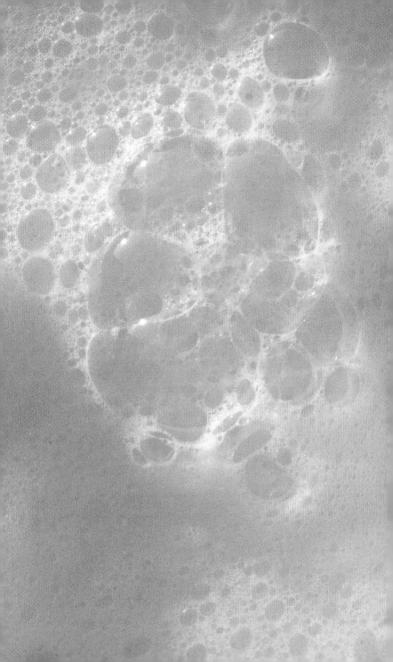